Bagels with the Bards
Bagelbard Anthology
No. 3

Also Available From

Ibbetson Street Press, Somerville, Massachusetts   2008

Bagels with the Bards — The Bagelbards Anthology No 1,
Edited by Molly Lynn Watt, Introduction by Tomas O'Leary
(2006) http://www.lulu.com/content/261048

Bagels with the Bards — Bagelbard Anthology No 2,
Edited by Molly Lynn Watt, Introduction by Afaa M. Weaver
(2007) http://www.lulu.com/content/729666

Bagels with the Bards
Bagelbard Anthology
No. 3

Edited by Molly Lynn Watt
Introduction by Regie O'Hare Gibson

Distributed by

Ibbetson Street Press
25 School Street
Somerville, MA
617-628-2313

ISCSPress.com
145 Foster Street
Littleton, MA 01460
978-633-3460

Lu.Lu.com

ISBN: 978-0-6152-0762-9

for Harris Gardner and Doug Holder

THANKS to

Bagel Bards for supporting this third anthology. For a flood of submissions followed by a flood of revisions. For caring about each word, each line, each off-rhyme, each beat. For joining cries and sighs into a reverberating volume of voice.

Au Bon Pain for a welcoming —and alternating —place for poets to hang on Saturday mornings

Backstare Poets for support on setting editorial policy and making necessary decisions

Tino Villanueva for the cover art

Regie O'Hare Gibson for the introduction

Mike Amado and **Irene Koronas** for wordcatching

Steve Glines for book design and production

Mignon Ariel King for being a second pair of proofing eyes

Dan Lynn Watt for being a second problem solver on glitches

 –Molly Lynn Watt, April 1, 2008

Oh bard, a bagel has become a poem.
  – Afaa Michael Weaver

Introduction

Bagel Bard – *noun*. **1.** A poet that is glazed and ring-shaped whose poetry has a tough, chewy texture usually made of leavened words and images dropped briefly into nearly boiling conversations on Saturday mornings— often baked to a golden brown. **2.** –*verb*. To come together in writership over breakfast. To laugh so hard at an irreverent statement that the sesame seeds of the bagel you've just eaten explode from your mouth like grenade shrapnel.

Welcome to the third *Bagelbard Anthology*. As some of you know (or can guess from the above definition) the Bagel Bards meet every Saturday morning at a designated spot. We breakfast in the original sense of eating, but also, because most of us are so busy working on our writing careers that we often find ourselves starved for great conversation. Well, the Bagel Bards breakfast hang is not only a place in which to do the aforementioned, but also to observe characters who themselves could be the subjects of poems and fiction.

> Dig:
> The PO-biz rainmaker with the Einstein Afro
> radiating from his head like so much silver light.
> The Cypriot grand dame who writes experimental
> hieroglyphs and writes down every funny or scathing
> quip (be careful what you say). The bespeckled cats
> with the jovial grins and clever poems that want to
> sneak behind the mind and give it a wedgie.
> The quiet-looking women with libraries in their mouths,
> their intellects so engaging you almost feel as though
> you're cheating on your spouse. There's the publisher
> dude.
> A quiet newspaper of a man with a wit so dry he shouldn't
> be near open flame. Then there's that Professor guy whose
> had as many books published as he's got fingers
> (now he's working on the toes).

Reading the third *Bagelbard Anthology* won't be exactly like sitting at the Bagel Bards table (by the way, you are welcome to join); but it will give you a glimpse into the motley characters who make *Bagel Bards* the institution it is becoming. So, thanks for joining us. All we ask is that you grab a cup of *chailattemochaspre ssodecaffeinatedorangejuice* and a bagel (you're looking thin).

– Regie O'Hare Gibson

*The genius of this anthology is as simple
and wholesome as a bagel...read it, and eat it.*
–Tomas O'Leary

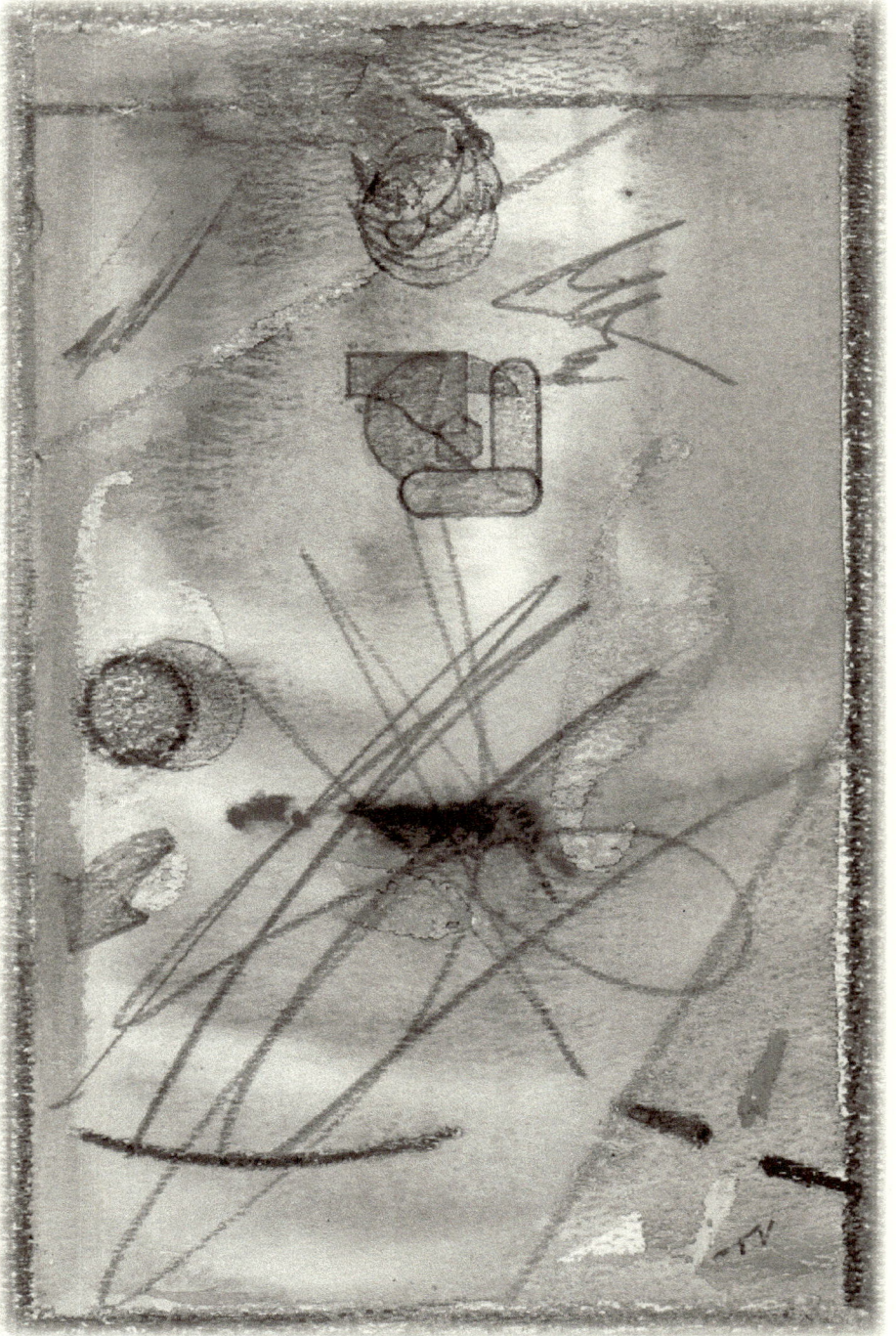

Flashpoints by Tino Villanueva

Contents

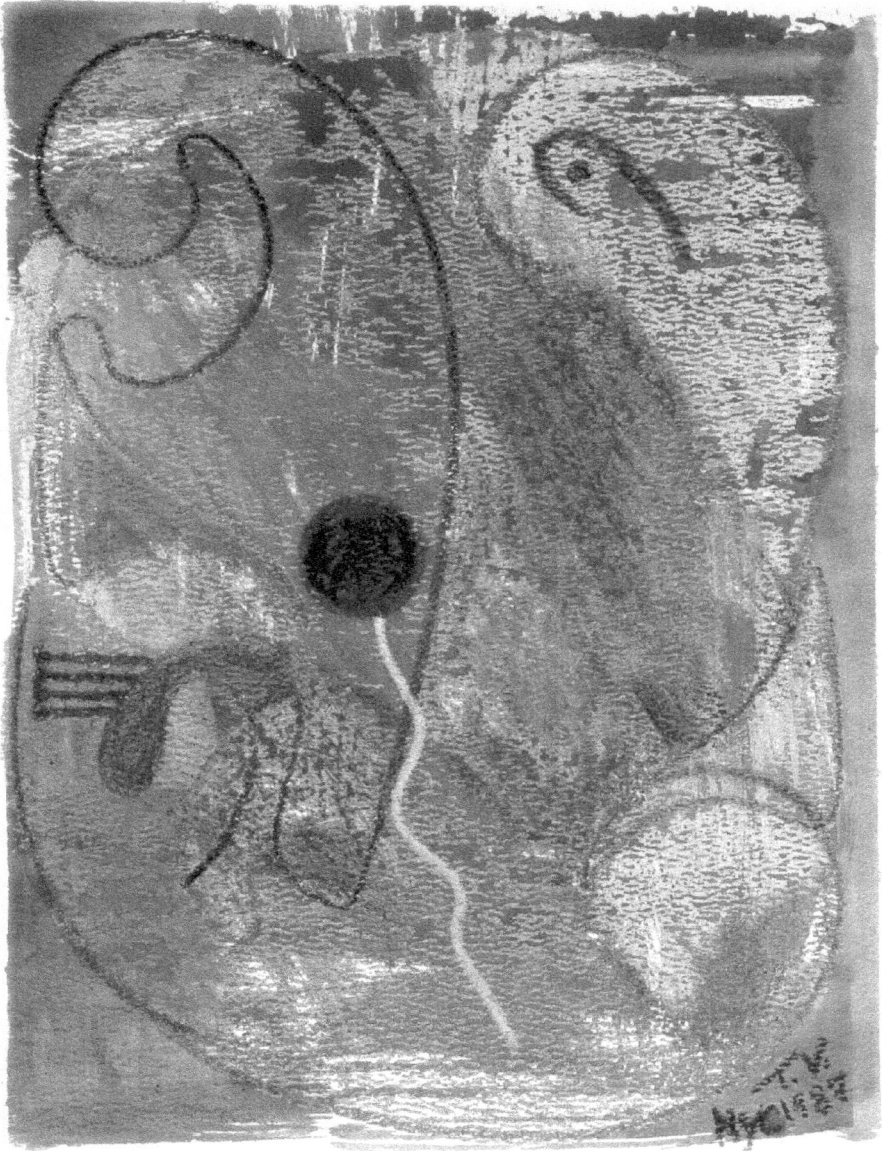

Looking for Miró By Tino Villanueva

A Good Day, Maybe

Last night's clogged clouds burst their borders.
Now, daylight drizzles into my somnolent mind.
I wonder what path I will wander today.
Rainbowed rays sink their shafts into my eyes.

I lazily ponder my rock-pounding fate,
to endure each twenty-four that
tiptoes into the room then body-slams
wakeful watchfulness into my brain.

The train carrying my passenger thoughts
is leaving the station, station, station.
I am not aboard, 'board, 'board.
I pray to G-d, as always, with no guarantees
that my voice will be heard past the silent stratosphere.

The Cosmos may find it a bit absurd
to reward the wishes of one small grain of sand
and may choose to ignore my will or won't.
Each hour is a trudge up a Sisyphean hill
until day's end bleeds the sunset
into the finger-stretching ocean crest.

You know how it feels when the earth rumbles.
It is not your stomach grumbling.
You understand that life is a slippery bar of soap,
and the ball of your left foot balances
on a brown banana peel.

Although part of me waits for the next blow to hit,
I always expect some sun to come of it.
So, if you say, "have a great day,"
I may reply, "I am a surviving willow that bends."

– *Harris Gardner*

A Union Soldier Has His Picture Taken

In June, I posed for a photograph with my Enfield at Matthew Brady's studio. My photograph was an ambrotype an image produced by light exposed over time to a colloidal solution on a glass plate. A million of these slightly brownish-red images would be made in the next four years.

Mine was typical.

A young man poses with his rifle. The soldier is new. The rifle is new. The uniform is clean. His face is full and despite a new beard, young. He looks serious, alert, ready. He can hold the pose long enough for the photograph the parade ground taught this even so, behind, looking like a third foot, is the base of an iron neck-stand to help those who have not endured drill remain still for the time needed to make an image. He stands on a linoleum floor which has a checkered pattern, like a kitchen floor. The cloth backdrop is dark. The soldier wears a .44 standard Army pistol, borrowed for the picture, a big US belt buckle, polished bright as the seven brass buttons down the front of his dark uniform. The kepi hat, cloth with slant top and short leather visor, provides some protection from rain, none from bullets, and is hot in summer and cold in winter. The photograph is used for a cartes-de-visite, a palm-sized image on cardboard, to be left, traded, cherished.

Ambrotypes will be put in embossed leather cases, displayed, kissed, wept over. The portrait is the last record for many families. Unnatural as the pictures are, they're the only part of the war the bereaved see. The rest they must imagine.

Mine shows a young man wary, proud, not overconfident.

Most of the men in these photographs, owing to the time they must sit or stand, look somber, lonely, isolated no one can hold a smile, artificial or not, for the time needed for an image to settle on the emulsion plate. The men leave no glimpse of personality, no revelation, no joke or nervous unease. They are alone. The portraits have a standard issue quality. They stare at fate.

– *Luke Salisbury*

A Second Chance

She said coming out of the hospital
Was like having a second chance
Blue kerchief around her head
Eyes tired, but not dead
She was calm, her pants were dragging
Under her shoes, shuffling down the street
What a beautiful day to exit from
A mental hospital, I agreed
The sun was burning its blessings
From the door to the floor
Our breaths melting as we spoke
I wanted to hug her but she was carrying
Half her life on her back
Her fingers wrapped in plastic bags
Too many clothes to keep track of –
And she was so calm though
Her eyes were just happy to gaze into the trees.

– *Deborah M. Priestly*

painting by Deborah M. Priestly

As Good As Dead

Morning consists of lying in bed
   with talk radio

Breakfast is a bowl of cereal
   day is a clerical job
      for a government agency

The apartment is always a mess
   debt is the rubber hand
      that slaps back

Doesn't own a television
   dinner is a bowl of cereal

Night consists of lying in bed
   with talk radio

Not much else to do
   except sleep
      repeat the day

Weekends in bed
   with talk radio
      listen, listen

No one to talk to

– *Zvi A. Sesling*

At The Café: Death By Cliché

"How are you?"
"Can't Complain."
"No one would listen anyway."

"And the wife?"
" Getting younger all the time."
"Apple of your eye?"
"Be with her till the day I die."

"Yeah, the world's your oyster,
You're the pearl before swine
We should dine out more often."
"Anytime."

"You asked how it's going
Well to be truthful
They say it's still growing."

"Look for the silver lining
Hope springs eternal,
Write that a hundred times
In your journal."

"But I fear
That I am dying."

"Cheer up,
What's the use of crying?"

"But
I am shooting from
The hip."

"Now, Now,
Stiff upper lip, and

Oh, yes…
Waiters always expect
 A twenty-percent tip."

– *Doug Holder*

At The Farmers' Market

Union Square
Somerville
he sits behind drums
totally focused
playing with his heart
making his music
while I sit
on a wooden bench
barely breathing
till I find
in the cracks
his jazzbeat
till I leave
my cracked heartbeat
so that I
may truly hear
this man's music.

– *Ann Carhart*

Ann Carhart

Between Snow And Leaf

Between snow and leaf
steals capricious April
stalking the fuzzy hills
switching her tail
baring her teeth
in a cheshire smile.

My hands ache to stroke her
feel her arch with pleasure
curl up and purr into green.

– Pamela Annas

Candle

Rings of smoke,
Buddha, burning by
my side,
he's waiting,
so am I

both melting to
the etha, waxen
tales, smoke
and stream
guide to the
floor, the
ceiling, and scream

melting to whom,
of whom dare
we speak,
droplets shadow
my dress, on
my skin
that is cream,
for life

my tears are
dry, the candle
that churns,
the light
that is offered,
and smells
as it burns,
no ash

to purify, to
cleanse, my woes
all disappear,
my dreams
they cascade, my
heart, not
gone, from you

– Jane Chakravarthy

Dalat, Vietnam

The light in Dalat rivals Paris.
Everyone wanted to be there.
First came the Chinese
bringing their wars, their opium.
Then came the French
with their army and their cooks.
Then the Americans
with their napalm, their agent orange.
There was one place of rest neither north nor south
where the monks lived with their saffron robes
and not a care who
traveled there, American or Viet Cong.
The monks sang their songs,
tapped their gongs, chanted for peace,
and on and on went the Vietnamese
riding bikes, planting tea, cooking,
mourning the dead.

– *Elizabeth Doran*

daylight savings time

today's daylight savings time
and of course i forgot forgot forgot to
change change change the clocks clocks
clocks last night so when i woke up
at 6 am i said go away go away go away to
the alarm clock but got up anyways today
is important i have to shop shop shop for holiday
presents so i got up out of bed bed bed and washed
up and ate and looked at my cell phone its automatic
clock read 5:15 holy moley i forgot forgot forgot its
daylight savings time i guess i already already already
saved time time time today.

– *pam rosenblatt*

ELENA (from the psych unit)

Elena flies to Guatemala in May
She's stooped over almost 90 degrees
We speak in Spanish undulations in the bathroom
As she runs cool water over her hands.
Not analytical English duals of psychiatrists
You take it on the chin, your head exploding

Elena, like a Twin Peaks cipher magical dream code
I follow the music:
La Primavera, mesa, the month of May
Flowers, Red and Yellow
Imaginary, bent over and unbreakably real.
When I leave the lavender walls seem to
Bloom again & I can escape.

– *Lo Galluccio*

Lo Galluccio

Exhausted
for Sandra Cisneros

In through my ears
Come images, projected
Against closed lids.
Night and day dreams merge,
Tempting me into nights
When I wish his breathing
Right here, my spent mind
Inspiring me to note, without budging,
That rain overflows the sills.

Even after I don't love him
Anymore in that passionate
No-other-man-will-do manner of madness,
Yearning to love lurks in the silence,
Mostly not at noon or dusk, just insomniac night,
Occasionally making floorboards creak,
Refrigerator catching its breath
Each time I peer inside.

Then it sighs at my pulling out
Only one pale ale, the pausing
Nibbles at a ball of cheese.
I try not to let the apartment
Get too very excited,
Hopeful, explaining the pitter-pat: it's only
The rain, and that's just fine again with me.

– *Mignon Ariel King*

Fieldtrip

The third-graders came to school
In warmest coats, mittens, and stocking caps.
Long scarves flapping
As they strode into the classroom.
Their teacher argued, "It's much too cold.
Wind chill ten below."
Along the way to Chinatown
They laughed, blew puffs of frosty air
Stopped to look in shop windows
Ran in to touch sizzling radiators.
At Golden Temple Ting's father greets them.
He smiles at reddened cheeks.
They wiggle up straight
Tuck in cloth napkins
As he graciously serves hot cakes and tea.

– *Barbara Thomas*

Gloria Mindock and Barbara Thomas at Luke Salisbury's party

Homeless

You'd never stay. The stars at night were your bedposts.
You must have built a mansion out of winter,
and the wind was the only resting place you'd take.

Hallways and open doors looked real in snowdrifts
making tiny shadows out of cold sparkles.
You'd never stay. The stars at night were your bedposts.

You did magic tricks, pulling a quarter
from behind my ear, once even an Oreo cookie. You believed in magic,
and the wind was the only resting place you'd take.

You'd expect for someone living on the street, that life
wouldn't be much fun, and sometimes you got a rooming house.
You'd never stay. The stars at night were your bedposts.

I wondered if you slept on subway grates in warm, billowing steam.
I wondered if you slept at all—you were always walking, walking,
and the wind was the only resting place you'd take.

I'd think of how you needed a pillow and a mug of hot cocoa,
but you found only the world and its storms.
You'd never stay. The stars at night were your bedposts,
and the wind was the only resting place you'd take.

– *Jessica Harman*

I Drop In At Downtown Wine And Liquors, Seeking Advice About A Decent White Wine To Accompany A Nice Piece Of Salmon...

for Curt and Janet

She wasn't, at first glance, remarkable:
dark hair in a jumble of curls,
off-the-shoulder peasant-style dress,
sweet, pale complexion. An Irish look
dark hair, shining grey eyes. But
all the way from neck to wrist, down each arm,
across what was visible of her chest.
A tattoo. The Pequod? The Charles W. Morgan?
Rebellion or a fashion statement?
I tried to imagine the reaction
when she showed up the first time
for a nice family dinner. Human scrimshaw.

– John J. Hildebidle

I *love*

getting high and riding my antique three-speed bike down the small hill from my campsite to the: Restrooms – Showers - No Washing Dishes - Paying Campers Only, dismounting and going into the well-kept recreational facilities and taking a hot, 50 cent, seven minute shower, arching my soapy back against the white tiles, rubbing my soapy front in the same spot, up and down, and up and then rinsed, standing, dripping in front of the first full-length mirror I've seen in weeks, gyrating my hips, mocking pin-up poses to myself and all god's good-looking men with a sense of the absurd, then wrapping my towel around, tying the knot between my breasts, standing outside in the sweet Santa Vidian air, finger drying my hair and imagining, unabashedly imagining guys in the campsite above eating fresh cooked meat and ogling me, and then taking off down the road, pale green nightgown fluttering against the spokes past Bonnie's trailer where from sundown till 11pm you can hear the best country music: Randi Travis, Willie Nelson, Hank Williams, Sr., then pulling up to my sweet "Bleu Belle," shushing the dogs reflexively, hopping off the bicycle, and turning, eyes closed, face upraised into a rare shaft of redwood forest sun.

– *Alyson Lie*

Jack Powers At Home

Going over his poems
for publication,
he picks the ones that
take the most from his
King James Bible,
deal with the source closest
to the source of all poems,
other books from favorites, friends
flipped through like yearbooks
without pictures,
his finger marking pages
like piecemeal petals
of ashen flowers
while visitors try
to leave annotations
in the dust topping his tomes.

– *Chad Parenteau*

Jack Powers
by an unknown photographer

January in Paris

Midnight and no train, Lazarus, Gare Saint Lazare
New Year's Eve, no trumpets, how bizarre
the last page of last year's news retracts
skitters nervously away down lonesome tracks
I am slightly drunk, you wobble in your course, my fallen star

We curse the rich man driving a warm car
I hide my secret knowledge I'm a lost passenger
going nowhere with you, last year's artifact
Midnight and no train, Lazarus, Gare Saint Lazare

Has the whole world left us here so far
from what we imagined we would be? Now what we are
is outdated, paupers, buried alive in fact
in this mausoleum station with dirt and worms and rats
I don't speak of what put us here, the scar
Midnight and no train, Lazarus, Gare Saint Lazare

– *Anne Brudevold*

Lament

Ringing the doorbell
on the precipice
to hell
Eyes like olives
hearts like stones
Will you or won't you
ever come home
again

"We will start the world over"
the voices told me
But under branches vines choke me
A prisoner to the lies
that the leaves
whisper in my ear
"You were never there"

"I WAS"
I scream
but my voice is void
A head full of isolated atomic bombs
like the ones they detonate
in the South Pacific
where the fish mutate
and develop three eyes
like myself
I am a fish with three eyes

A hopeless in between afternoon
sitting on the porch
lack of caffeine hurts
I can't help but remember
when my life was much worse

– *Shannon O'Connor*

Leaving Wishes

It's not the Western Wall,
urgent wishes on a thousand
bits of paper in the shadowed spaces
between the sunwarmed stones.

No, I'm in Philadelphia,
alone as the restaurant begins to fill,
next to me a space in the exposed
brick wall and, deep between the bricks,
a paper, yellowed, folded small.
I tease it out, open it: it is blank.
And I, who cannot leave a star
unwished on, write one small word,
retrace the paper's folds,
replace it in its niche, brush the
salting of brick dust from the
tablecloth, and wonder who
would have missed the chance
to wish, or could not trust
a wish to solid writing?

Then I see the wall is peppered with
openings, each big enough to hold
a wish. I could have wished again,
again, given some away. There are
clefts enough for everyone, the couple
reaching hands across the table,
the friends leaned in and whispering—
everyone around me talking, eating, unaware
they were so close to all that they could wish for.

– *Ellen Steinbaum*

Limits

It is hard to observe
Boundaries in midair
Blindfolded
The pull of gravity
Like words
Cannot be second guessed.

If you grab onto the hand
Of a friend
A few feet above ground
It will turn out
To be a laugh over dinner

If this time
Without warning
It should be the canyon
Of no return
Please keep your fists
Balled up
In the pockets of your jeans

For old times sake
Endure
The free fall
Prepare for the laugh
All the way down

– *Linda Larson*

$$\lim_{x \to 0} \frac{1}{|x|} = \infty$$

Listening To Jane Hirshfield

The reading is at seven
and it's raining outside
windy, cold.

I skip dinner, run to the car
drive too fast down glistening streets.

Lucky this time
a parking spot close to the door.

I hang up my raincoat,
sit on a hard plastic chair—

and we are in a Zen garden
uncluttered
calm
with a cat
a horse
the immense beauty of a beating heart—

Branches tap against the window.

– *Patricia Brodie*

Love letter to a sanitation worker

All week I build a mess to fill
the drum, the hollow bin—
burnt toast and crumbs and oatmeal lumps,
bits of chips and cherry pits,
cabbage shreds, a gnawed-on rib,
my candy wraps and *TV Guide*, my blahs,
my ashes, dregs, and grounds, my infant sins—
they all go in.

I cart the refuse
to the curb to rendezvous—
my stink, your win.

Motor roils,
gears to metal grind.
I stay inside and peek
through dusty blinds
to catch the din. I watch
you boost and dump and haul
the fetid shrine.

I am the maiden of good waste!
Maybe next time, dear, I'll load
both barrels with these runny dreams—
vintage from this lonesome
kitchen sink of mine.

– *Varsha Kukafka*

Lower Than The Grass

At the needle exchange I tested
an Indian man for HIV. He said
he found us through a pamphlet
at his doctor's office. No needle

use he said; not even drugs; just
multiple sexual partners. He was
so straight that I thought his chance
of coming back positive was

lower than the grass. Which was
why I won't be surprised when
he is the first of my clients
to show antibodies. I felt like

he was lying about half the things
he told me and I was probably
half right. But that's no reason
to buy the ticket. Some of us

get our cards punched; others
go over Niagara Falls in a barrel,
the lights on the water are impartial,
almost like the Gods we pray to.

Some of us are meant to float.
The rest of us swim like stones.

– *Marc D. Goldfinger*

Maria

Pale eyelids, dark brown eyes—searching for escape.
What will it be today? A machete or a
gun that dooms your face into that final photo.

Little girl, you had no choice but to
grow up quickly. In your nine years of life,
someone should have told you the
whole world isn't like this.

When you walked up to the mass grave,
you saw your Mama. Twisted body,
dried blood, and decaying skin.
You crawled into the stench and held her.
No tears flowed—just a determination from
a girl wanting her Mama back.

Staying too long, you played dead as the
soldiers passed by laughing at what they did.
With fear gripping your tongue, you didn't scream.
Your bravery, something to tell later.

When you left the grave, the image stayed in your eyes as well
as a piece of cloth from your Mama's dress.
See her smile as you cooked supper together.
Hear her laugh as you played.
Hear her tell you not to wander too far away.
All these things a Mother does.
The cloth now pressed close to you.

Another family saved you, escaping
on a long and sometimes frightening trip.
In southern Illinois, refuge was taken. And as I
listened to your story, I took your hands
as you finally cried.

– *Gloria Mindock*

Mirage

Crescent moon
Icicle curtained
Window.

Crystal thorned
Cavern of sight.
partial,
reflected,

light.

Mirror eyes
starlit,
glimmering,

night.

empty cavern
dark dwelling

Men live here.

White desert,
Cold city.

– *Matt Rosenthal*

Nemo of the Rails

The railroading *zanni* and journeyman
in wait on the platform, notebook in hand,
writes "no one belongs in a train station."
So he waits, his bag of masks shoulder slung,
for the window that frames his companion's
tipping hat.
                    Embarking for Providence,
their boots pound the bricks of Empire Street
or Lower East Side, Manhattan concrete
when out of service stations send them back-
tracking through Chinatown and Soho to
joisted wood stages of Bowery art spaces
peddling canvas patches of silk-screened haiku
of Nemo's autumn railroad wanderings.
Piercing the beholder's eye, he is the
no one who belongs in a train station.

– *Ian Thal*

Ian Thal
by Elizabeth Schweber Doles

Nine Clicks

Click—the flipped switch sound of lights on or out.
In rapid succession? Turn from the usher
at the switch, clear the lobby.

Click click—a shotgun loading as heard on TV.
The drama's brought home
unfolding
in the darkened family room.

Click click click—a dead ignition
switch and go
virtually gaming
in alien dungeons
on cold red-drenched moons.

Click click—"What's happened?"
Artificial optimizing
just before all evidence of
it disappears. "Oh, nothing."

Click—everything's now in place to make
the latest scene. This takes a walkthrough
or a riot, depending on the light.

– *Dale Patterson*

Now That I'm In Spain

(Reflections of Madrid, summer 1969)

They have lined my tongue against a concrete,
diaphanous wall:

    the many rifles at the cross roads
    where the careful traffic goes,
    and general eyes are blazing
    from behind
    Don Quixote at the Plaza de España.

In a crossfire of glances
I stroll La Gran Vía wondering if he
who burst *¡FUEGO!* at Federico's blood
has his voice still—
that blast of truth keeps ringing in my ear.

On Sundays I examine El Rastro.
Its threatening 1936 rust is ever rugged.
Better to sit at sidewalk cafés to conjecture
the origins of tourists.
The only time I part my lips is to sip sangria;
then once in my secret heights I embrace the dark,
and hope no one knocks at the door.

– *Tino Villanueva*

Old Reverie, New Prayer

My pen remembers not to know where it's going.
The choir sounds a placid sea.
I throw my line.

I catch from memory's current
that zestful sister of the cloth
who bothered me erotically most bedtimes
when I was in fifth grade.

She wore full habit in those dark-age days
but had a strut that seemed to raise her hemline
from shoe-length to mid-calf.

In wildest dreams I never saw her naked:
not totally, that is, but always buffed
with bits of black and white
in special places I'd caress
with prayerful eyes.

In class she held us all in thrall:
beauty and laughter magnified the Lord,
her sudden song, her little dance of glee!
I learned alertly, chastely.

Today I love her all anew.
I pray Amen for her, not out of habit
but because the Mass is ending.

Ghost, teacher, friend, beloved
in sublime and godly ways:
God knows how flesh redeems us ever
as the spirit plays!

– *Tomas O'Leary*

On Cambridge Common

Students hustle by but do not see him
alone on the park bench taking a smoke
Years ago he was a student on his way to somewhere
Now he spends his days on the Common
his silver hair pulled out of the way in a pony-tail
always the same frayed jeans and shirt
gray sneakers tied with string
A canvas case patched with duct tape sits beside him
he lifts out a battered 12-string guitar
its bridge stressed out from years of percussive picking—
glances at the faint autographs on its leather back strap
Josh White, Guy Carawan, Pete Seeger, Tony Saletan—
places his still-burning cigarette between two strings
adjusts the tuning pegs, strums to find a key
hums as his feet tap out the beat and sings
This world is not my home, I'm just a-passing through...

His lips curl into a smile around the sounds
as he sings to a galaxy of ghosts
He is not worrying about sifting through trash cans
for discarded chips, half-eaten sandwiches
nor finding a place to sleep on a bench, behind a bush
or with some young woman happening his way
willing to share her dorm bed for a night of song
Tomorrow he will drift off to another bench
shrouded in the proud tradition of protest
to rage against hard times, lost causes, corrupt bosses
mine disasters, union strikes, unjust wars, parted lovers
not thinking of the wife and babies he left behind
He pauses for a nip from his monogrammed flask
The angels beckon me, through heaven's open door
And I don't feel at home in this world anymore...

– Molly Lynn Watt

On Moody Street

Up the hill the common's statues looked
Down past the railway crossing at the river
With the technical dignity of a doctor
Ignoring the patient's winces to feel the sprain,

Apprehensive yet searching, with resignation
In the discovery that alarms us. Sat to
Paper mazes, START HERE on the outer
Wall was a deception to lead you

To dead-ends. Somewhere I'd learned to pencil
The center tracing my way back out of it
And so each of the gatekeeper's questions should be
Answered with evasion. It was his grin

For being amused, not frown for being solved
That saved you from the nightmares of usurping
Duncan's cups. But putting that together
Had me on my knees washing my face

In river water for so long I came
To own it, as the birds own the dynamics
Of the sky, forever to make our fire
Contrived and awkward and wasteful in comparison.

The briefer my sleight, the more resonant the silence,
Hallmark of margins to write wishes in
Because there is no formulating
The elusive laws in progress meant to make

The near and further lullabies all equal.

– *Michael Todd Steffen*

Pale imitation of a poem
for Jack Powers

Inspiration on the back, side,
inside flap of an old utility bill
three poems to be read once
then placed in a filing system
only a fireman could love:

"Old man rises
for Madonna with child
noisy, smelly, subway car
modern manger, god bless,
god bless."

"Screams to the Almighty
murder the infidel
blasphemous
pox upon your house
... all your houses ....
And we wonder why God is silent?"

"Bus travelers in common
a conversation stricken
at our destination when
we become fearful, alone again.
Why? When we had
so much in common?"

– Steve Glines

Rain Drop Blues

This blue blues
  poem is written
    in a thunderstorm
      with me, a drop of rain, sliding down
        outside this wind-swept window pane,
       a liquid abstract painting
      of water beads running, stopping,
    swept sideways, then in circles,
   going down to you, this shimmering puddle
at the bottom of the window sill;

Certain I'll fall to your willful smile,
  you track all of my slip-sliding moves
    to these elements blues, propelled
      as I am by wind, lit up on a celestial canvas
       by lightning, as you confidently whisper,
       it is the way of droplets and puddles to merge.
      But, I persevere, believing
    that even the smallest among us
  can align our wills
to alter life's course, by resisting

with all our might, the wind,
  yielding when we must,
    and riding sound waves of thunder
     using lightning's beams as our guide.
      Then we could hit the bottom   alone
     and wait, with a virgin's anticipation,
    the fall to us of that first drop, knowing
   that we, too, can embrace the cyclical calls
  to brave a tidal wave
of fully living

– *Nathaniel H. Mayes, Jr.*

river chat

the river looked solemn
when i said
"what happened to the breath i saved.
i wanted to let off steam.
the walk is all uphill.
on my own mountaintop
i'm king without a dream,
keeping still."

the river said
"don't try.
you need beans and beef."

"but," i said, " i only have 20 dollars
'til monday.
oh well, maybe i can buy
what i want to say.
good breathing needs good feed."

an echo
comes from the willow.
with an amen.
and from the river,
an emanation,
a deep sigh of relief.

– *Martha Boss*

Romare and August ©

Of Romare Bearden and August Wilson

Standing at the door and knocking - in his mind
Standing at the door without knocking in reality

In the reality of 'the stoop' the poet stands at the door without knocking.

Two floors above, a figure, solitary. (It is Romare.)

Solitary, unknowing, the other man, older,

stands at his window

surveying the stoops of his neighbors

Unseeing the reluctant young poet on his own

But seeing . . .

Seeing what he all ways saw,

Over a half century of life on these stoops in piano-journeys and jazz-journeys.

Ships and chains. Railroadchains, bloodchains. Chains broken-mirror jagged and dripping with plasma. Cataclysmic, brooding chains, chains vibrating 'like something terrible', chains like terrible big hands.

Hands large enough to hold every thing and every body.

Master Romare . . . standing there, at his window.

Seeing all, one humongouscollagemontage before his seeingeyes

Looking at the invisible poet on his stoop, lacking the spirit,

But holding the promise.

– *Lolita Paiewonsky*

Rosa Parks Died Today
a villanelle for racial equality

Move to the back of the bus
Coloreds will never have their way
Rosa sat for all of us.

Hear the White men, as they cuss
Do not cross what they might say
Move to the back of the bus.

Seats of color show disgust
Racist clans rule the day
Rosa sat for all of us.

Whites govern, don't create a fuss
But dreams of equality won't go away
Move to the back of the bus.

Men were lynched in trees they'd truss
Then set on fire with dry hay
Rosa sat for all of us.

For a year, we walked through dust
Reverend King told us to pray
Move to the back of the bus
Rosa sat for all of us.

– Elizabeth Leonard

Sketch #14
(from Sketches of Lake Attitash)

All is still
at end of storm.
Lake has lost
its wind-driven waves.
A sunset so silent
only the surface
remembers its hues.
Night slips in slowly
as song of peepers
in distant marsh
stirs memories of evenings
in early Spring.

– Lainie Senechal

Spring in Rome

Spring.
The clerk returns the key to the desk
I have emptied my shoes of sand
And slide my bare feet across the warm stones
In the alley a cat eats a mackerel
Her claws like steel
And her eyes glinting like hot copper
Spring.
Nuns parade past the trattoria
Easter is past, supplications fall dead
Sin smells in the air like honey grass
At fountains, slums, and from windows above
Laundry dries in the hot sunny wind
Spring.
Brown-legged kids run on cobblestones past cars
Past urinals, past vendor's stalls, past markets, past school
Ladies wear large hats and sit at cafés
With open knees and shaded eyes
They sharpen their claws
Wear their eye patches
And get ready to
Dangle their heads over the cliff.

– *Julia Carlson*

"Sweet Cold, Chicago"

Wipers
smear grease
from a city
that sleeps

Chicago,
I've waited for her
to embrace, instead
it's a cold bed
in the darkness
bringing loneliness
in the middle of night…
If I could find blues
only on the radio,
that is all talk

so buzz by
3 AM
It's raining,
once again
I roll down my window
and Chicago
can spit back

– *Timothy Gager*

10,000,000 Elvis Impersonators Can't Be Sane

Eight year-old   with an Elvis swivel,

Lip cocked   in parody,   involuntarily.

Gold Lamet   tailored suit,

Greased up pompadour.

Singing Dion, doo-wop and

You ain't nothin' but a . . .

Every shuffle choreographed,   his dad

In the background: shake left,

then right,   that is right.

Dad is his manager:

Forty-something,   pot-bellied,   bald,

Hips don't swivel anymore . . .

He says: Ain't it nice to see the young ones

            pick up the torch!

Translation:

I'm so lucky to see my dream live

– *Mike Amado*

The After-Birth of Tragedy
After a conversation with an ex

      Being with you
was the vestal opening of new
books whose unread tongues
licked paper-cuts on my eyes

      Being with you
was incensed night wafting days
in anger & smoke, you:
a phenomenology of Geist's
graceful as Hegel, Kant, dance

      Being with you
was like being a one winged jack
ass carpet munching the crabbed
grass between Kali's legs
   was
    like watching Pandora unlock
a box of Promethean livers, let me be
clear, I really hate being un-under
stood, how can i say this?

      Being with you
was both religious & philosophic,
was like being an Evangelical
                   Polytheistic
                    Nietzchean:
I just always
had a sinking
   faith
that more than one
god was dead

– *Regie O'Hare Gibson*

The Alter Sun

Fear does not speak
except where battered woman shows
her wounds to that battered-other.
Silence is a ghost. Mist covers her bruises.
O mother sun! This is how
she wants to shine.

Fear is alive. It runs.
Words echo in their ears
to awaken old prejudices, step aside.
Candor reveals her still innocence.
O mother moon! This is how
she wants to die:

into the juices of her mom's belly
where peace reigns
no noises,
no sketches,
of what it could have been.

— *Beatriz Alba del Rio*

To you E. V.:
the woman-child who nobody protected until you withered from
this Earth.

The Boy Jesus

Mom, I want to know who my father is.
You've told me more than once
Joe is not my father. Well, who is?

Please. I'm not a baby. I know how it's done.
The chickens and the camels. The fishes and the flies.
Somewhere I must have a real father.

Oh Mom, not that old son-of-God line again.
We're all children of God.
I'm twelve years old – I need to know –

What kind of man is inside me?
Dead-beat dad or prince? Beggar or slave-owner?
Straightforward or secretive?

Half my friends are in mixed families.
Samaritans and Jews. Romans and Greeks.
If he's not a Jew – OK, OK! I'm sorry.

If you were secretly married – even
if you weren't – a lot of girls these days
are not virgins when they marry –

Don't get mad. It's not about you.
Your past – whatever you've done –
Mom, I forgive you.

It's not even about Joe.
He's good to me – he's a great step-dad.
But he is not my *father*.

It's about who I am. I'm almost a man
but only half a person. Mom, help me
become a complete human being.

– *Llyn Clague*

The Daring Dance of Fall

It's a burlesque arabesque
as the wind grows high
and the rain flies,
though they especially shimmy
for the sun.

They'll drive you mad
as they drop their leaves,
first one then two then
hundreds
till they're bare—

leaving brown rags
for the rakes to wear!

– Barbara Bialick

(Originally published by *Freestyle Vision*)

(The) Moon Goddess

White goddess of the night
Lovely the mask of pearl
That smites my timid blood.

I am too frail to bear
Such pain-full fire.
Kindly leave me rage and burn
Under lesser light.

– *Walter Howard*

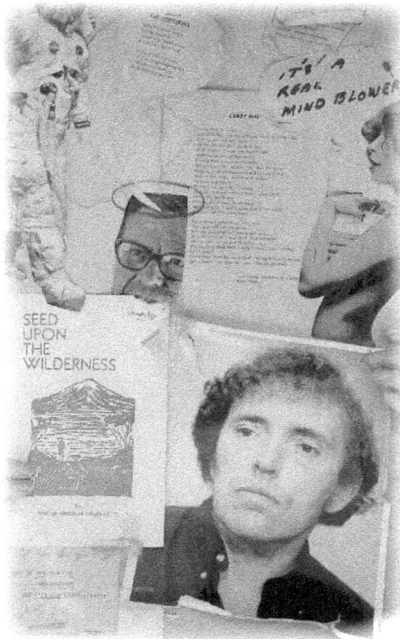

Walter Howard as a young man

the race for one sentence

each down splattering her impartiality
his finger tip walls folded on greasy lines

it's best to hold her cake

her gigantic walking across his body mass
sometimes
red just to give edge its turn
another turn a third turn
time is personal motions
her hands holding
every anniversary as every proof past
last

he hunts through the frosting
racing
rolling in
square pieces like slop in dirty places
his open alarm hunger gets closer
just when the pendulum taste needs cutting

perhaps he overturns
turnover little keepsakes and turntable sugar charged drinks
he downs ouzo by the sea
baking gray red dots
his knock underground
and
tunnel winds heave batter soaks the half grounded other side

she clumps thumps snatches tittering procession
dread lock arms
they smooth out their differences
pass plates

– *Irene Koronas*

To Emily Dickinson

Staggering like a cormorant
through water tension
you slung yourself
into air darker than bone.
The world to the top of the hill
and no faster.
You were a votive bat
blinking out of small caves
a torch fusing pollen
and horse hair
a marsh drowned
in the thaws of April.
You were housebound.
You were driven to sleet.
Parsley nicked your ankles
as a funeral procession tipped
into that field where forever
rolled its profit and its blight.
Outside your window,
gnats still collide with your arithmetic.
At school there was a clock
and a missal with ribbons.
You turned on the sour heel
of your theology
and stared them down.

– *Tom Daley*

Originally published in *Alehouse*

Victory Garden

Was it in forty-three
Or forty-four, or both?
The world was wrapped in war.
I watched my father march
Down Foster Street. He had
A spade, a hoe, a rake
To make a garden in
A winter skated field
Drying under the spring's
Incendiary bursts
Of flowers over this
Five-o'clock shadow man
Who taught Shakespeare and caught
The scent and feel of earth
Running soft in his hands.
He lined a string between
Two sticks, defined shallow
Trenches where he prepared
His ground. He would tear the
Picture packets at their
Corner, spreading seeds in
Tidy rows covered like
Combat dead in wartime
Cemeteries. Carrots
And radishes, string beans,
Lettuce, peppers and peas,
A neighborhood of food,
Of coming victory
Imagined, summer's feast
Renewed, and then released
As autumn memory.

– *Philip E. Burnham, Jr.*

Virginia Spring

Left and right
magnolias,
mauve-white, drop their petals.

In the middle,
out through an arch of pale grey stone—
perfect for home viewing, double-framed—
the bodies come.

Their bearers cup them
under armpits, knees,
shuffling the sag of lifelessness
away:

out the doors,
down the steps,
thirty-one times.

In the pockets of the dead,
cell phones ring.

– *Abbott Ikeler*

Weigh

The ecstasy of being eaten is more than the fear
in the teased air between pine needles and red lilacs
where we take turns shooting through the thin circles
made on the edge of the hawk's wings, the tiny space
it cannot come back to except to arc up again,
navigate, draw once more the line from her eye

to a place where we have no escape. It is the way
the heat pumps the whole mountain until it is drunk
with sun, so full of it that its stone heart melts
to make its own waters trickle down the slopes
to gather in the gullies, softening the ground
for the snakes who have lost their envy of dragons.

It is the teeth, sometimes the sweet juice of the mouth,
the belly flesh of the jaws, the eyes falling back
into themselves with relief from hunger. We think
ourselves invisible but still the lure of going in
is greater than the fear of never coming out, so we give
ourselves to the joy of change. Time always ignites

again, even from the great time of nothing that spat
the world from *the long sleep*, a hunger
like this way we ache to know desire lives in the eye.

– Afaa Michael Weaver

Previously published in *Under the Rock Umbrella*

Word Catcher Poem ONE

this word catcher has been on vacation, lounging on nothing and eating off the blank landscape of laziness. I'm tan and ready to get back to what is being said by our fellow bagel babes and dunking dudes. our sun worshiping gentle feuds fuel the pages we leaf through.

we try to find precious shade under umbrellas and by the shadow of poets already seated in davis square. our cream cheese breath floats over our heads. we often disagree with each other about politics, interpretations and what poetry is or is not, but, we keep coming back because we are a doughy tribe of scribes looking for companionship and we all understand it is always one bagel at a time, one discussion. one can give response to one who needs our attention; a poet's (dog) loss, poet's concern about travel to a warring country, a new poet, trying to fit into an established group.

this word catcher is back from justified margarines and is buttering up her bread

words caught:

did you notice the typo

I saw another 5 somewhere

sits not gonna come

after the 3rd draft, you get drunk

depressing frequency

coffee ground conversations

I've got the blue cheese repetitions

– *irene koronas*

Word Catcher Poem TWO

We were interviewed by a writer from 'what's up magazine'; she's writing an article on 'spoken word' poets. I had to look up on the computer what that phrase means. I thought most poets spoke their words before an audience. Of course, I now know the term means poetry oriented toward performance. Most of the Bagel Bards spoke with her and their words seem to tickle her fancy. Most of the poets did not behave themselves and that is what is expected of a bunch of ruckus dramatic word manipulators. For sure, she was entertained by us and may come back to participate in our tight knit community of writers.

Words caught:

I'm too pompous to believe I'm pompous

Notable un-notables

I like being a baby because you get free service

Pass the torn book please

Bad weeks are great for poetry

When things get tough you write a lot of stuff

Our lady of ladies

He hit the ground falling

My dental tools come in handy

It's so loud you can't hear the raunchy

– *irene koronas*

Wordcatcher Poem THREE
August 18th '07 or "Picketing Ted Hughes' Grave"

Morning breeze delivered a trace of autumn.
Terse like the crisp pages turning of the first edition
copy of "Crow" that I just purchased. Everyone's repelled.
One Bard was ready to grab a torch and a pitchfork exclaiming:
"Ted Hughes killed Sylvia Plath!" There were even shouts of
picketing Ted H's grave   (if only he had one!)
Somewhere, the wind brandishes carrion love songs, the ashes
of Ted Hughes form a palace of skulls for Sexton to savor,
saying, "Think hot! You Hot ticket!" as his soul is thrown to the
oven.

The Bards' ambiguity for the work of Ted Hughes was thick.
Some say he was an exceptional poet, others say, "Just an Artist"
and he possessed an ego like Cookie Monster . . .It's always
hungry.

But "Them's that have 'um, wears 'um".

Ted H. would be nothing without Sylvia the same way Elvis
Presley was the Colonel's marionette. Elvis Presley was, after all,
the first Boy Band product. Then, It was on to Luke's house to
decide what is the best Rock & Roll song. My pick? It ain't Elvis!

– Mike Amado

Word Catcher Poem FOUR

September 29th—The coming autumn was felt in the lazy morning wind, blowing summer afar and in its place, leaving conversations of foot fetishes and broadsides that "lack substance." Besides our dismantling of the Mr. Rogers enigma, we discussed how a poet should be a vessel for universal expression.

We are here to absorb, process and circulate that expression. Then we started talking about the "Food Chain" of life and its interaction in the poets' world. It seems poets are after the metaphoric equivalent of "food, shelter, money." but of course, there's little of the last out there so I'm stating the obvious.

Words caught:
She's a good person to look at
Don't judge me, judge my art!
Mr. Rogers wasn't a pervert
Deconstructing Mr. Rogers
Is the pervert here?
Let the thing pass
The fashion police of the Bagelbards

– *Mike Amado*

About the Contributors

All poets in this anthology are active Bagel Bards, coming together on Saturday mornings to sip coffee, network and schmooze. The group has a fluid identity, boosts member's accomplishments at readings and by publishing. Most were published in previous Bagelbard anthologies. Below is a sprinkling of individual biographic notes.

• **Beatriz Alba del Rio,** born in Argentina, is a bilingual poet, lawyer and mediator living in Cambridge. She won 1st Prize in the 2002 *Octavio Paz International Poetry* Contest, 3rd Prize in the 2003 *Pablo Neruda International Poetry Contest,* 1st in the 2004 *Cambridge Poetry award.* Her poem *Black Crows* was nominated best "female love poem." • **Mike Amado** is a performance poet who does lyrical tomes attuned to the social and semi-political. He is the host of three poetry venues in Massachusetts. He is an online reviewer for *Rattle Magazine* and the Boston Area Small Press and Poetry Scene. • **Pamela Annas** has poems forthcoming in *Ibbetson Street, The Northwoods Anthology*, and *Hunger and Thirst*, an anthology from City Works Press. • **Barbara Bialick** is the author of the new chapbook *Time Leaves*, published by Ibbetson Street Press. • **Martha Boss** is a painter and a poet. Her poems have appeared in *The Register, Spare Change, The Aurorean, and Arts Media.* Her paintings are in numerous collections and are shown annually at the *Fort Point Open Studios.* • **Patricia Brodie**'s poems have appeared in *The Comstock Review, The Lyric, California Quarterly, The Pedestal, Phoebe* and many other journals; her chapbook, *The American Wives Club* (Ibbetson Street Press 2006). • **Anne Brudevold** has a chapbook, *Luminal Wait,* and is founding editor of Eden Waters Press. • **Philip E. Burnham, Jr.** has been writing poetry for half a century and has four books of poetry including *A Careful Scattering* (Cervena Barva Press, 2007), and his book *Housekeeping* was featured on NPR's *Writers Almanac* • **Ann Carhart** is a Cambridge poet and psychologist who admits to being born in Brooklyn and falling in love with poetry while living in the Village. She has a book, *Sanctus! Sanctus! Sanctus!* and her poems appear in the anthologies, *Cries of the Spirit, Heat City Review,* 2nd *Earth's Daughters.* • **Julia Carlson's** chapbook *The Turn of the Century* was published in 2007 by Cloudkeeper

Press. • **Jane Chakravarthy** is a visual artist and poet and resides in Somerville, Massachusetts. • **Llyn Clague** has a second book, *ON BECOMING A POET FULL TIME*, from Pure Heart Press. See www.llynclague.com • **Tom Daley** teaches poetry and memoir writing at the Boston Center for Adult Education, the Online School of Poetry and Lexington Community Education. His poetry credits include *Harvard Review, Prairie Schooner, 32 Poems, Poetry Ireland Review* and *Del Sol Review,* his chapbook is *Canticles and Inventories.* • **Elizabeth Doran** is published in the journal *Poesies* and *Spare Change News*. Elizabeth has read at many venues in Greater Boston including Borders Books, The Newton Free Library, Stone Soup. •**Timothy Gager** had his hand in founding The Dire Literary Series, The Somerville News Writers Festival and the *Heat City Literary Review*. The fiction editor of *The Wilderness House Literary Review* lives on www. timothygager.com. • **Lo Galluccio** is a poet and vocal artist whose work appears in *Abramelin Magazine* and at www.strangeroad. com. Her forthcoming EP/CD is *The Dream of Life*. Check her out at http://www.myspace.com/lolagalluccio. • **Harris Gardner** has three books: *Chalice of Eros* (with Lainie Senechal), *Lest They Become* and *Among Us*. Harris is the founder of Boston National Poetry Month Festival and Tapestry of Voices. He was nominated for a Pushcart Prize and received honorable mention for the Boyle-Farber Prize. • **Regie O'Hare Gibson,** with an MFA from New England College, has taught and performed in seven countries including Cuba. His work appeared in *The Harvard Divinity Bulletin, The Iowa Review*, NYU's *Renaissance Noir, Cave Canem's Gathering Ground Anthology*, Guild Complex's *Powerlines Anthology, The Spoken Word Revolution*, and *Poetry Magazine*. Gibson is a fellow at Black Earth Institute and head of the fusion ensemble Synesthesia. • **Steve Glines** comes from a long line of failed and petty literati. His mother was a journalist, his daughter a copywriter. His grandfather, who wrote over 20 books, once said, "If all else fails you can always write a book." Steve has written 7, designs many others, and is founder of the *Wilderness House Literary Review*. • **Marc D. Goldfinger** writes because he is compelled by an Unseen God. He was published by the *Ibbetson Street Press, Poesies, The Boston Poet* and others and is the poetry editor of *Spare Change News*. • **Jessica Harman** has an essay on the source of poetry forthcoming in *The*

Iconoclast. • **John Hildebidle**, is an English teacher at MIT. His most recent collection, *DEFINING ABSENCE*, was published in Ireland by Salmon Publishing, which will issue another gathering, *SIGNS, TRANSLATIONS* in late March. • **Doug Holder** is the founder of the Ibbetson Street Press. His recent poetry and articles appeared in *Rattle, Cafe Review, Caesura, PRESA, Poesy, Boston Literary Magazine*, and others. He was nominated for two Pushcart Awards in 2007. • **Walter Howard** was included in Robert Pinsky's *America's Favorite Poems*. His poetry has appeared in *Boston Poet Journal, Ibbetson Street, Spoonful*, and others. He read for Tapestry of Voices at the Boston National Poetry Festival, Stone Soup Poets and throughout New England. • **Abbott Ikeler** teaches communication at Emerson College in Boston. His book *Outpost* was published by Ibbetson Street Press 2007, and a short story appeared in *Eden Waters Press' Home Anthology*, 2007. • **Varsha Kukafka**'s short stories and poems appeared in *Painted Bride Quarterly, First Intensity, Wilderness House Literary Review, Lyrical Ballads, swankwriting.com, and Hacks*. • **Irene Koronas**, with many chapbooks to her credit, is the poetry editor for the *Wilderness House Literary Review* and she loves Saturday mornings with the Bagel Bards. • **Mignon Ariel King** is a Simmons College English degree holding, Aerosmith lovin', Sam Adams swigging, Charles River roving, rabid Red Sox rootin', native Bostonian bachelor woman. • **Linda Larson**'s *Washing the Stones* was published by Ibbetson Street Press in August, 2007. • **Elizabeth Leonard** is a psychologist who teaches at Harvard Medical School. Her poetry relates to issues concerning loss, recovery and social justice. • **Alyson Lie** works with *Peaceworks Magazine*. • **Nathaniel H. Mayes, Jr.**, gets exposure at the Cambridge Cantab Lounge and other local venues. He is completing his first chapbook. • **Gloria Mindock** is editor of Cervena Barva Press and the *Istanbul Literary Review*. Her book, *Blood Soaked Dresses*, was published by Ibbetson Street Press. • **Shannon O'Connor** has published fiction in *Up Dare* and *Chord* and poetry and fiction in *The Wilderness House Literary Review*. • **Tomas O'Leary** has published two books of poetry, *Fool at the Funeral* and *The Devil Take a Crooked House*, both from Lynx House Press. • **Lolita Paiewonsky** writes librettos, drama, fiction and poetry. She presented poetry with classical and jazz music, choreography, and exhibits it as poetâge. She featured at Tapestry of Voices at Borders Books, Soaring Places Videos and

Fireside Readings and is working on an historical novel, *Aleksandr and Anatoly*, based on Pushkin. • **Chad Parenteau**'s new chapbook is *Discarded: Poems for My Apartments* from Cervena Barva Press. He helps host the long-running Stone Soup Poetry series founded by Jack Powers. • **Dale Patterson** counts syllables 28 per stanza in Somerville, MA and writes prose for the Boston Public Library Foundation. • **Deborah M. Priestly** runs the Out of the Blue Art Gallery of Cambridge and hosts the Open Bark Candelite Poetry venue. Her last published book of poetry was *The Woman Has A Voice*. • **Pam Rosenblatt** is the Assistant Editor of *the new renaissance* and an arts contributor for *The Somerville News*. She has been published in *Lyrical Somerville* (The Somerville News) and the *Ibbetson Street Update*. • **Matt Rosenthal**'s poetry has appeared in *Somerville News*, *Wilderness House Literary Review* and other places. His poem *Ethereal* was displayed in the window of the Grolier Poetry Book Shop.
• **Luke Salisbury** is the author of the cult classic *The Answer Is Baseball*, and three works of fiction, *The Cleveland Indian*, *Blue Eden*, and *Hollywood and Sunset*. • **Lainie Senechal** co-authored two volumes of poetry, *Chalice of Eros* with Harris Gardner and *Naiad's Lantern* with her sisters. Her poetry appears in the anthology *City of Poets*. She is co-producer of the Culture of Peace, an exhibit connected to the U.N. mandate for a decade of peace and helped create The Peace Garden in Egleston Square.
• **Zvi A. Sesling** had poems published in numerous magazines, received First Prize in the Reuben Rose International Poetry Competition 2007 and was selected to read his poetry at New England/Pen. • **Ellen Steinbaum** writes the *City Type Column* appearing in the *Boston Globe Weekly* section and has a new book of poetry forthcoming. • **Michael Todd Steffan** won the Ibbetson Street Press Poetry Award in 2007. • **Ian Thal** is a mime, *commedia dell'arte* actor, puppeteer and student of kathak, whose poetry appeared in *Becoming Fire: Spiritual Writings from Rising Generations*, *Tokens: Contemporary Poetry of the Subway*, and *Boom! For Real*. • **Barbara Thomas** has a chapbook, *Seduced by Sighs of Trees*, Cloudkeeper Press. • **Tino Villanueva**'s *Scene from the Movie GIANT* (Willimantic: Curbstone Press, 1993) won a 1994 American Book Award. • **Molly Lynn Watt** has a book of poems, *Shadow People* (Ibbetson Street Press 2007) and a CD, *George & Ruth: Songs and Letters of the Spanish Civil War*. Her writing appears in dozens of journals and anthologies, she gave

the Jeff Male memorial reading at the Joiner Center (2007), and she curates the *Fireside Readings* • **Afaa Michael Weaver** has ten collections of poetry, two professional theater productions, short fiction in journals and anthologies, and has given hundreds of readings in the U.S., Great Britain, France, China and Taiwan. He was a Pew Fellow, the first Elder of Cave Canem and is a Professor of English at Simmons College. •

Notes on the design of the book:

body type is 12 pt. Classical Garamond
ᖇeadline type is 18 pt. Dolphin Bold

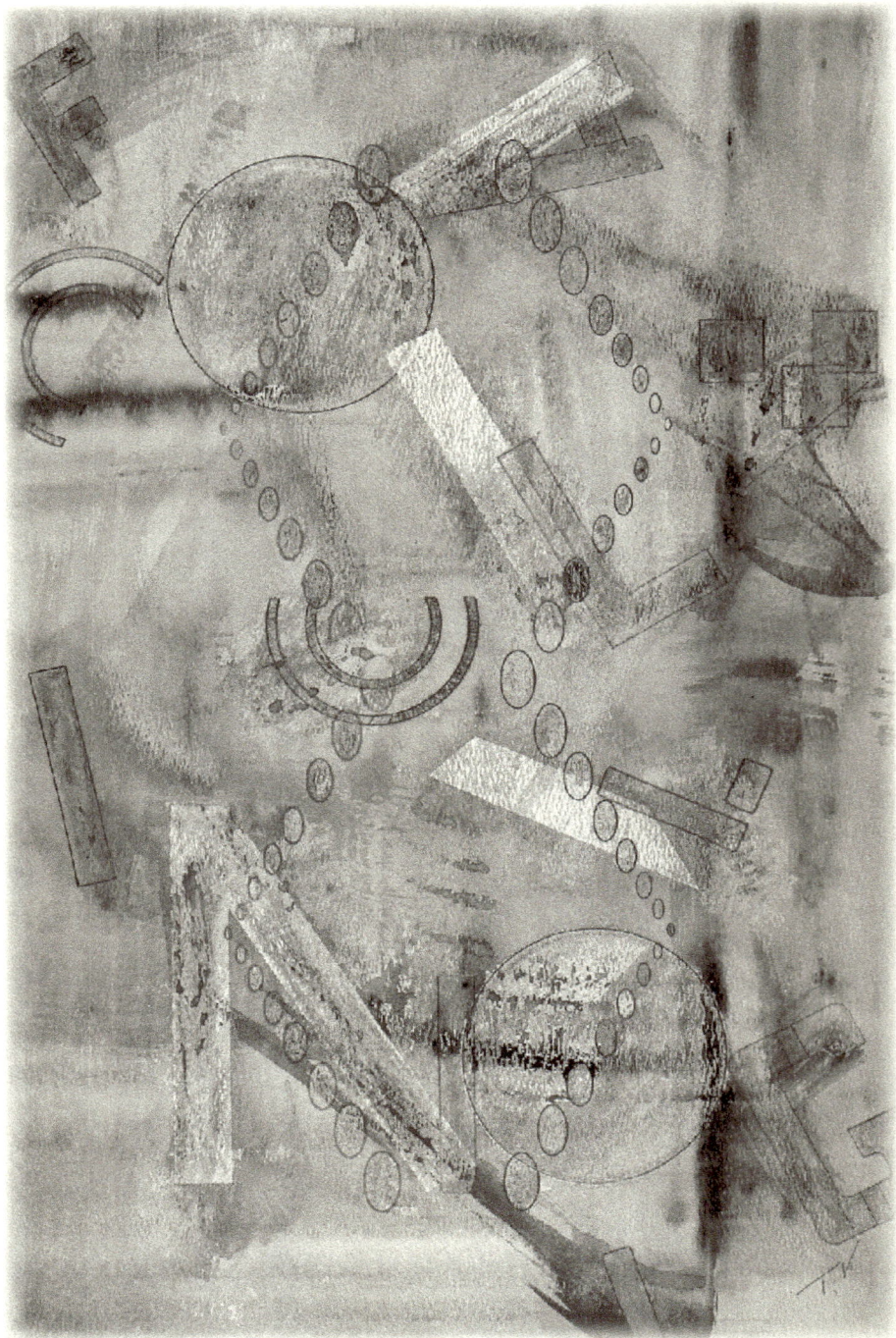

Falling into Place by Tino Villanueva

Ibbetson Street Books

IBBETSON STREET MAGAZINE (Published twice a year in November and June: $7/issue, $13/2 issues.) □Issue 22 has an interview with the late poet Sarah Hannah, author of "Longing Distance" (Tupelo Press). Also new poetry from Jade Sylvan, Eleanor Goodman, Lyn Lifshin, Marc Goldfinger and others. Issue 22 was featured in "Verse Daily."

TIME LEAVES by Barbara Bialick ($8.50) "Barbara Bialick's poems leave the reader with a sad/sweet acknowledgment of the passage of time. Her work is generously laced with humor, irony, and a peaceful acceptance of what is, and what is to come. This is a poetry collection for all seasons; to read when you are old and when you are young." — Doug Holder, Arts Editor, The Somerville News.

MANUFACTURING AMERICA: POEMS FROM THE FACTORY FLOOR by Lisa Beatman ($15) Susan Eisenberg, author of Blind Spot, says, "Manufacturing America bears witness to the lyrical life of a factory and the individuals who inhabit it at the start-up of the 21st-century. Lisa Beatman adds the stories of immigrant workers, heard through the ear of a poet on site to teach literacy skills, to the growing literature of work poetry." CONFESSIONS Selected and Edited by Llyn Clague ($10) "Nuggets of irony in the ore of verse!"

AWAKENINGS by Richard Wilhelm ($15) "In Richard Wilhelm's powerful free-verse, sonorous, image-tapestried first collection, the mature poet takes us through a remarkable series of awakenings, most of them to profound interconnections between himself and primordial riches of the natural world—half-buried treasures that glimmer with mystery, ecstasy, and the divine, and that contemporary humans have to a great extent lost touch with in their techno-industrial materialistic lives." Douglas Worth / author of "Catch The Light" (Higganum Hill)

SELECTED POETRY (Vol. 2) by Susie D. ($5) More poetry with an edge from journalist, and author Susie Davidson. Davidson is a reporter for the Jewish Advocate and other newspapers, and the author of the critically acclaimed anthology "I Refused to Die..." a compilation of 30 stories of local Boston-area Holocaust survivors and liberating soldiers of World War II."

JEWISH LIFE IN GERMANY - PAST, PRESENT AND FUTURE:
OUR TEN-DAY SEMINAR by Susie Davidson ($5) This new book
by Susie Davidson chronicles an Aug. 20-31, 2006 seminar she
attended along with five other Bostonians as a guest of the Federal
Republic of Germany and the German Consulate of Boston. The
group visited many memorial sites, met with German dignitaries
and government officials, attended synagogue and traveled to sites
of interest relevant to German Jewish history. Photos and text.
100 pp.

BLOOD SOAKED DRESSES by Gloria Mindock ($13.50) In her
fascinating poem cycle, Gloria Mindock jolts back into memory
the roots of El Salvador's present day violence. Mindock coaxes
to the page the voices of the dead who lie, less in peace, than in
restless obsession with the atrocities they suffered. She brings
forth as well the voices of the living who seem startled to find
that they died somewhere between the horrors they witnessed and
the grave they have yet to lie down in. Blood Soaked Dresses is
a beautiful, harrowing first book. - Catherine Sasanov author of
Traditions of Bread and Violence (Four Way Books).

FROM MIST TO SHADOW: POEMS by Robert K. Johnson
($12) Fred Marchant (Director of the Poetry Center at
Suffolk University) writes of Johnson's work: "His is an art of
transparency, an art in which language through its own devices
becomes nearly invisible and what is seen through the scrim is
usually an epiphany... The ordinary life is under the poet's gaze
transformed into something approaching the sacred..."

SONATINA by Johnmichael Simon ($13) "Discords, misses and
tangles, are all addressed and folded into the Sonatina while the
carousel revolves. What this book accomplishes for us is the vision
of all events meshing in the music of life, the bizarre just another
octave, the sweet and miraculous all plucked appropriately in
reprise and return: "the clouds and God are all that exist and
the music, the music."   Katherine L. Gordon, author, editor,
publisher, literary critic.

WASHING THE STONES by Linda Larson. Photos by Karen C.
Davis and Rob Rusk. ($10) Howard Zinn noted activist, historian
and authors says of Larsen's collection: "I am very moved by
Linda Larson's poems. They are about gliding gulls and young
love, and a homeless woman up against a tree all the stuff of life,
straight from the heart." Linda Larsen is the former editor of
Spare Change News.

SELF PORTRAIT DRAWN FROM MANY: 65 POEMS FOR 65 YEARS by Irene Koronas ($11.95) Irene receives the smallest whispers - a scrap of paper, a single word, a passing impression and shows us reflections of the infinite, the holy, the human. Her writing evokes ancient dream-time meditations only to return to the mundane details (polish my toe nails) that bring us back to the particular, the present. Her poems are peopled by all sorts of characters; scholars, theologians, children, philosophers, musicians, painters, gamblers, activists, artists, monks, saints, lovers, fathers, mothers, and on. Irene invites us, with this collection of poems, to think about who we are in relation to others - to see ourselves in many different shoes. Ultimately it is an act of great empathy and great imagination. These poems are never didactic, often prophetic, always provocative.

OUTPOST - A COLLECTION OF POEMS by Abbott Ikeler ($16.50) In Ikeler's poetry, we watch the footprints of dancing maidens disappear at the edge of shore. We watch the beasts of the woods watching a wild thing cutting wood. We trace the DNA of Jove back to the scenes of his crimes. These poems combine the observation of a Robert Frost walking a bleak New England landscape, the pessimism of a Matthew Arnold listening to the sea above Dover Beach, and the wit of an Alexander Pope, as Ikeler encounters the paradox of living a life consistently shadowed by death. Spare in expression but unsparing in their vision, the poems manifest a rare fusion of intelligence and imagination. Order from: http://www.lulu.com

CYCLAMENS AND SWORDS AND OTHER POEMS ABOUT THE LAND OF ISRAEL by Helen Bar Lev and John Michael Simon. Poems and Paintings ($36) The achingly beautiful cover of timeless trees, earth, flowers and rock, is redolent of Israel's destiny. This little land, so hallowed in human history, seems the literary and spiritual core of existence to most of humanity. If strife is ever present here, how can there ever be the peace of ancient promise? This land seems to symbolize the eternal quest for harmony where forces of turmoil march ceaselessly. Bar-Lev and Simon explore this theme for us. Cyclamens and Swords will become a treasured classic, echoing as it does so fluently, the longing, fearing and questing that marks these troubled times. Can be ordered on: http://www.lulu.com

SHADOW PEOPLE - Poems by Molly Lynn Watt. ($14) Fred Marchant (Author of "Full Moon" and Director of the Poetry Center at Suffolk University in Boston) writes of Watt's book:

"Shadow People begins far away and takes us on a journey home. We move from the Mendenhall Glacier in Alaska to the Redline in Boston....We begin as observers but by the end of the book we have joined with Molly Watt in the dance of her life, and our own." Can be ordered on: http://www.lulu.com .

LOUISA SOLANO & THE GROLIER POETRY BOOK SHOP - Edited by Doug Holder & Steve Glines. ($10) This is a collection of anecdotes by poets who have patronized the famed Grolier Poetry Book Shop in Harvard Square over the years. Also: an exclusive interview with Louisa Solano, the former owner, who recounts her experiences with Allen Ginsberg, Jack Kerouac, Robert Lowell, Donald Hall and others. Contributors include: Afaa Michael Weaver, Deborah M. Priestly, Linda Haviland Conte, Lyn Lifshin and other poets. Also order through:http://www.lulu.com/content/353454 .

THE AMERICAN WIVES CLUB - Patricia Brodie. ($5) "Patricia Brodie's poems are warm and witty with wonderful surprises for the enchanted reader. Her poems reflect a life of love, friendship and travel, of eucalyptus trees, found treasures of the sea, and the bittersweet memories of home and family. They sing." Victor Howes, past president, New England Poetry Club.

BAGELS WITH THE BARDS: THE BAGELBARDS ANTHOLOGY No. 1 - Edited by Molly Lynn Watt. ($7) An anthology of poetry by the "Bagelbards" a group of poets who met in Harvard Square, Cambridge (now in Davis Square, Somerville, Mass.) every Saturday morning over bagels. Included in the anthology: Patricia Brodie, Ann Carhart, Irene Koronas, Marc D. Goldfinger, Beatriz Alba Del-Rio, Mike Amado, Varsha Kukfaka, Lo Galluccio, James Foritano, Matt Rosenthal, Doug Holder, Julia Carlson, Gloria Mindock, Philip E. Burnham, Walter Howard, Robert K. Johnson, Steve Glines, Tino Villanueva, Clara Diebold, Deborah M. Priestly, Afaa Michael Weaver, Molly Lynn Watt, Barbara Bialick, Tomas O'Leary, and Robert K. Johnson.

WAY, WAY OFF THE ROAD: THE MEMOIRS OF THE INVISIBLE MAN - Hugh Fox. ($15) This book has anecdotes from 40 years in the small press, by none other than poet, anthropologist, critic and publisher Hugh Fox. In this book, Fox gives it to you straight with no chaser about such people and things as : COSMEP, "Pushcart Emporium," Len Fulton, A.D. Winans, Charles Bukowski, Lyn Lifshin, Harry Smith, Tuli Kufenberg, Richard Kostelantz, Menke Katz, Junior's Deli in Brooklyn, Allen Ginsberg, "The Last Great Poetry Pow Wow,"

Richard Nason, Dotson Rader, Diane Wakoski, Ghost Dance Magazine, William Wantling, "The Living Underground," and so much more... This is a beautiful perfect bound edition, edited and designed by Steve Glines, with an introduction by Doug Holder. "Hugh Fox is the most distinguished man of alternative letters of our time." Richard Kostelantz author of "A Dictionary of the Avant-Gardes."

SANCTUS! SANCTUS! SANCTUS! - Ann Carhart. ($8) Ann Carhart considers herself an old local Cambridge, Mass. poet and psychologist. In this poetry collection she traces her life as a young girl, her marriage, her divorce, and her resurrection... A powerful collection from a veteran of life.

HOUSEKEEPING: POEMS OUT OF THE ORDINARY - Philip E. Burnham Jr. ($8) - "Philip E. Burnham's third collection, places him firmly in the company of Rhina P. Espaillat, Donald Hall, Brendan Galvin, and other equally rare talent. These poems cover the gambit of loss, through death, of his wife... This collection like a good marriage, is 'to have and to hold.'" Harris Gardner (Tapestry of Voices).

I REFUSED TO DIE: STORIES OF BOSTON-AREA HOLOCAUST SURVIVORS AND SOLDIERS WHO LIBERATED THE CONCENTRATION CAMPS OF WORLD WAR II - Susie Davidson. ($18) "In writing this book, Susie Davidson is advancing the eternal message of the most significant event in Jewish history. The Holocaust was an essential element in the establishment of the State of Israel, which reserves an official national day for honoring its memory. Its lessons are the most profound and the most crucial in the creation of our modern Jewish identity. Susie's effort to document its story and its survivors is to be supported and is greatly appreciated." Hillel Newman, Consul of Israel to New England.

HOT RAIN - Lo Galluccio. ($5) These poems are about love, loss, identity and just the language out of which they are made. Lo Galluccio is a popular Jazz vocalist and poet residing in Cambridge, Mass. (Published by the Singing Bone Press an imprint of Ibbetson Street.)

LIVING IT - Joanna Nealon. ($10) A new book of poetry by a poet who is blind. Acclaimed poet X.J. Kennedy wrote of this poetry collection:" Living It is a spellbinding book.... I haven't read autobiographical poems this stark, harrowing and memorable since Robert Lowell's 'Life Studies....'"

THE WOMAN HAS A VOICE - Deborah Priestly. ($10) Rose
Gardina publisher of the "Boston Girls Guide" writes of this
book: "Deborah M. Priestly's poetry is moving, deep and
passionate. She has captured the depth that every woman feels at
some point in their lives with such meaning and grace. She truly is
one of Boston's great treasures of talent." Illustrated by Lauren M.
Geraghty. Edited by Lynne Sticklor.

SELECTED POETRY - Susie D. ($3) A book of provocative
poetry by Boston-area journalist, political activist and poet Susie
D. Susie's poetry is right-in-your face, as it rails against injustice,
and the modern malaise society finds itself mired in.

SAILING FROM BOSTON: POEMS OF LOSS AND
REMEMBRANCE - Philip E. Burnham, Jr. ($8) Burnham pens
a collection in memory of his wife Louise Hassel Burnham.
Burnham is a graduate of Harvard College, and was a former
American Vice Counsel stationed in Marseille, France. His first
collection of poetry was My Neighbor Adam published in 2003.

FAIRY TALES AND MISDEMEANORS - Jennifer Matthews.
($5) This is a first poetry collection by this well-known Boston-
area vocalist/poet. Matthews "strings words with wings" in both
her songs and her poetry. No wonder she is often described
as "the next Patti Smith." Check out her website http://www.
jennifermatthews.com

STONE SOUP ANTHOLOGY - Stone Soup Poets, Inc. ($7)
This joint project by Ibbetson Street and Stone Soup Poets, is
a collection of poetry by poets who regularly attend and or
contribute to Stone Soup in some way. Stone Soup, founded by
Jack Powers, has been a venue of reading and publishing for over
thirty years in the Boston area.

THE SAME CORNER OF THE BAR -Tim Gager. ($5) Gager is
the founder of the successful reading series Dire Reader, housed
at Cambridge's Out of the Blue Gallery. This collection is a hard-
hitting look at the war between the sexes, divorce, drugs and
booze, and parenthood.

ON EITHER SIDE OF THE CHARLES - Doug Holder. ($4)
Mike Basinski, Assistant Curator of the Poetry and Rare Books
Collection of the University Libraries at Buffalo writes of this
book: "...when I read his works, it was with great gobs of joy that
I felt such bubbling joy at his very easy way of capturing instances
of common and making them high holy."

RELATIONSHIPS - Marc Goldfinger. ($10) This is former Spare Change's News editor, Marc Goldfinger's first collection of poetry to be released by Ibbetson Street. Goldfinger, a well-known street poet in Cambridge, writes of his hardscrabble milieu, and the relationships that bind and break.

A KOAN FOR SAMSARA - Linda Lerner ($5) These poems, written between late June 1991 and early 2003, arranged more or less chronologically, tell a love story, the kind that, if you're lucky, happens once. Once only.

LEST THEY BECOME - Harris Gardner ($6) " 'Lest They Become' is an exploration of the spiritual, emotional, and physical comforts and complexities of roots by a tireless contributor to the poetry community." Ellen Steinbaum (Boston Globe Columnist and author of Afterwords).

IN THE BAR APOCALYPSE NOW - Gary Duehr ($4) This collection of poetry deals with the 60's and the aftermath. Duehr is an award wining poet from Somerville, Ma., and co-director of The Invisible Cities Group, a performance group based in the Boston area.

SLOW AS A POEM - Linda Haviland Conte ($8) 23 poems written with an observing eye, and a quiet and spiritually reflective voice. Conte brings tender seriousness, as well as wry humor, to the subjects of domesticity and motherhood.

SMALL WORLD - Poems by Jonathan Roses ($5) This is Roses' first collection of poetry that Hugh Fox describes as "... a refreshing break from Beat/Post-Beat tough-guy street poetry... Simply a kind of wonder at what is...genuinely moving."

BOSTON: A LONG POEM - Hugh Fox, Photos/Art: Richard Wilhelm ($2) A trip to Boston serves as a jumping-off point for a man's recollection of his life and times.

THE LATEST NEWS - Robert K. Johnson, Illustrations: Richard Wilhelm ($4) A native New Yorker's journey to Sept. 11.

THE LIFE OF ALL WORLDS - Marc Widershien ($10, $1 p&h) A memoir of Boston in the 40's, 50's and 60's. Jack Powers, founder of Stone Soup Poets wrote: "This brilliant energized portrait of a once-ago urban neighborhood throbs with affection and detail. Kudos!"

CITY OF POETS/18 BOSTON VOICES - Editors, Don DiVecchio, Doug Holder, Richard Wilhelm. ($10). This is an anthology of 18 Boston poets of diverse background. Lawrence Ferlinghetti wrote: " Bravo to the Boston poets for hearing the Muse loud and clear!" Cover art by Richard Wilhelm.

THE INACESSIBILITY OF THE CREATOR - Jack Powers.($3) A collection by Boston Beat poet Jack Powers. Ed Chaberek of Superior Poetry News called Jack, " A powerful poetry presence!"

DREAMS AT THE AU BON PAIN - Doug Holder. ($3) Poems composed during a hot Summer, while sitting at this sprawling Harvard Square cafe. Mike Basinski wrote of Doug Holder, " All a poet...he is among the the vertebra that holds the Boston and eastern Mass. poetry community up to snuff." Art by Richard Wilhelm.

WAKING IN A COLD SWEAT- Doug Holder. ($4) A book of 3 A.M. night sweats...the dark night of the soul.

EARTH SONG - Don DiVecchio-($3)- This is a collection of poetry by the poetry editor of Spare Change Newspaper. It deals with the 70's, activism, poverty, gender issues, and childhood. Pictures by Divecchio and Richard Wilhelm.

POEMS FROM 42ND STREET - Rufus Goodwin- ($6)- Poems of the street...poems that find the poet. Jon Galassi wrote: " I found much to admire in both the poems and the drawings."

THE BERKSHIRE POLISH BAR/And Other Blue Collar Poems - Ed Chaberek-($2)- A collection of poetry by the editor of SUPERIOR POETRY NEWS. This collection deals with a working class town in New England in the 1950's. Illustrations by Richard Wilhelm.

POEMS FOR THE POET, Workingman, and Downtrodden- A.D.Winans-($3)- This collection was praised by the Chiron review...it deals with the streets of SanFrancisco as this veteran poet sees it. Art work by Richard Wilhelm.

LEAVING ONLY IMPRESSIONS-Dianne Robitaille- ($2) A collection by an editor of the Ibbetson Street Press. Robitaille's poetry deals with the passing moment as it dissolves into the ether. Photos by Doug Holder.

WALK OUT - Ed Meek-($4)- Poems about the beauty and horror of nature, in and around a placid suburb of Boston. Art and photos, Richard Wilhelm.

ANGEL OF DEATH - Hugh Fox-($4) - A collection of poetry that deals with mortality... illustrations by Richard Wilhelm.

PRAYERS ON A TENEMENT ROOFTOP -Ed Galing-($2)- Poems of the Lower East Side of NYC during the 1920's. Art and photos by Doug Holder.

These books can be ordered via mail:

Ibbetson St. Press,
25 School Street
Somerville, Ma. 02143
or call (617) 628-2313.

§